CHARLEMAGNE
A SONG OF GESTURES

John Gery

PLUMBERS INK BOOKS
Cerrillos, New Mexico

FIRST EDITION, 1983

Library of Congress Catalog Card Number: 83-60255

ISBN: 0-935684-06-9

Grateful acknowledgement is made to the following in which some of the poems first appeared.

Berkeley Poetry Review: The Flight from Europe (Parts I and II); Confederates' Park

Chicago Literary Review: In Nice

Chicago Review: Casting the Rear Guard: A Vision (as Casting the Rear Bumper Guard); Charlemagne at Macy's

Greenfield Review: Breakfast: Off the Sunnyside Exit

Literary Review: The Daughter of Desiderius; Before the Banquet (as Charlemagne's Third Daughter)

Michigan Quarterly Review: Monks Compleynt

Poet Lore: The Organ in Aachen Cathedral

South Dakota Review: Edifice Rex (Parts I–III); Milwaukee's Clean (as Charlemagne in Milwaukee); The Macula

Cover: Albrecht Dürer, *Kaiser Karl der Grosse* (1512), reproduced by permission of the German National Museum, Nuremburg, West Germany.

for family, mentors and friends

I cannot be absolutely sure these happenings will in fact be
described by anyone else. I have therefore decided that it
would be better to record these events myself for the informa-
tion of posterity, even though there is chance that they may
be repeated in other histories.

—Einhard, *Vita Caroli*

CHARLEMAGNE
A SONG OF GESTURES

CASTING THE REAR GUARD: A VISION

With his Bestiary and his Bible
Charlemagne rides down West End
and on to Lincoln Tunnel
                    where I wait
(without a steed to travel by)
inside a tollbooth, no blanket,
though Roland offers a cigarette,
                    the bell rings,
on a cold night that tastes good.

We break rye bread between us,
Roland and I. The skyscrapers
sway like stallions.
                    The bell rings,
another Rambler leaves the city,
a bus for San Francisco,
we spread hot coffee between us
                    and smoke fumes,
staining bloodless Durendal.

We are waiting, we are about to leave.
Rain appears in the headlights,
wet tires screech,
                    the bell rings,
Roland lays a heavy hand on Oliphant,
turns over the motor, pays his toll,
and backs his car into the Hudson:
                    "Charlemagne!
Where the hell are you?"

I

Of Charlemayn fain would I hear you speak
He's very old, a hard life 'his has been;
Two hundred years and more I know he's seen;
In lands so many his body he's fatigued.

—Song of Roland

PEPIN

Pepin was a magistrate; Pepin
registered his father's words in his vest
pocket. On an ordinary day
after shining his suit, after breakfast,
just before the sun rose, galloping
first cut into the fresh air, he would pause
to nod at the horses at their hay
and give the dog water to dip his paws

in. Pepin was never late to work,
though the dusky road to Prüm stretched through five
thick forest leagues, Pepin persevered.
Through basilisks and griffins, he'd arrive,
chain mail still spotless, and set to work
on the pandects, *lex loci,* and money.
He'd a head for business. He was reared
to adhere to discipline. It's funny

to think back, when he was young and wild:
"Pepin the Short, Terror of Acquitaine"
who once led a band of marauders
from Aix-la-Chapelle as far south as Spain.
Scourge of the Saracens, Pepin styled
his troupe after mad Godefrid, the Dane,
until he said: "I long for my daughters,
their well-being, and my son Charlemagne!"

VIRELAY: THE PALACE LIBRARY

In this library's cupola sphere
Charlemagne recites from
the *Aeneid,* or Homer, by ear,
or Bede's John Chrysostom.

Not the meaning but delicate hums
he hears, and his patched face
starts to soften, as music becomes
the mother to his race.

"It's the poet's rhetorical grace,"
he says, "not what he sings,
that I've wanted so long to embrace.
Songs command change as kings

command Rome, Troy, Byzantium, Aachen.
Decor, their belvedere;
rude desire, their queen; their awaking,
the poet chanticleer."

THE DAUGHTER OF DESIDERIUS

Your pale Italian hair,
Desiderata, your full
mustachioed lips, your
railing wrists and
narrow ghostly hips,
Desiderata, Desiderata,

wrapped in my cushions
and furs, trapped there,
a downy fox, I struggle
the chamber, the bed, the
bellows, my arms and legs,
your narrow breasts,
Desiderata,

Desiderata, my face
in the veils of your hands,
many hours by many spirits,
by my shield and arrows,
I lusted on you, your cheeks,
your bony knees, your eyes

never broken, Desiderata,
dear tremulous Desiderata,
so much in vain.

MONKS COMPLEYNT

Twenty-eight Bibles from cover to cover,
two for each of Charlemagne's children, and not
a lost soul's chance in Hell they'll survive this war
or the next plague. Thirty-six years: my fingers
curl from dipping styluses in india ink
and pressing damask or gold into parchment.
I've written The Creation twenty-eight times,
twenty-eight times I've nailed Christ to the Cross.
I am told that during the Apocalypse
no one will read Bibles. I can accept that.

Yes, some parts of this world simply have to die,
like my work, to make room for what comes after.
On hot afternoons when I tend the garden
my robe fades to a brown August landscape
with sheep running through it, grazing the straw flax,
while blue sheep dogs who guide them to Hungary
cool themselves in the shade of the balusters
holding up the rails, holding up the cloisters,
holding up the columns which support the church.

Last Sunday after Vespers I remembered
our evenings at home when I was a child.
After supper I'd take Josef out to run,
first through the monastery, then in the fields.
We'd turn in at Dothan's barn, panting, panting
from running, but before we'd fall asleep,
I'd often remove my torn jerkin and stroke
his brown coat — such a lovely coat it was, yes,
but some parts of this world simply have to die,

and sometimes I'd remove my shirt, quietly,
to touch the sleeping, sighing dog close to me,
shrinking in the heat, his eyes like closed Bibles.
Twenty-eight Bibles. No one will remember
when I dipped myself in the blood of a dog.

THE ABUL ABBAS LETTERS

> *This Arab Abdullah . . . sought the friendship
> of the Frank and related to Charlemagne the
> wonders of Baghdad, where the brazen lions
> roared like organs. And Charlemagne dis-
> patched envoys to Baghdad to ask for the
> gift of an elephant.*
>
> —*Harold Lamb*

I

I write because we cannot see
each other, nor ensure peace,
nor conduct private intercourse.

I want to entertain your grace
and appeal to you over distance,
but I offer only crude greetings,

no evidence of authority, no
reason behind the impulse, no
threats or ultimatums, only that

my people, Christian people, will battle
for the Byzantine, turn jewels into ash.
The fierce dogs of Empire march east.

I want nothing but your pleasure
and, perhaps, a sign of your pleasure,
though I fear Jerusalem is sovereign

here where we enjoy none of your
sweet unguents, nor gilded sandals,
know nothing of the strength of elephants.

II

I am seeking in this quagmire a king
or new union—
        O write to me that you care,
        that your silence is a sign.
I have gone three days without water,
without a word,
and my stomach pains increase
by the hours marked on your waterclock:
        You are my last pearl
        and you cannot vanish,
        you cannot ignore this
        war between us.

I am surrounded by my properties
and what children
        survive by our marriage, ours
        the vital bond, the most dear.
Lost to the Bulgars and the Avars
without a fight
I am alone and long for a word.
Can there be no break in the mountainsides,
        no rise in the fog
        to catch a glimpse of you
        touching a silver brush
        to your black hair?

I send you my best messenger.
        With him a Frisian cloak
        and six Spanish mules.
I await your reply. *Hasten it.*

III

We are pleased with the beast and you
are responsible for this new grey hulk
stumping our northernmost territories.
I say: Why have you done this to me?

He eats the thatch off our houses,
brutally tears up tree roots and fences
and desecrates our trim cathedral
gardens, honking like a battle horn.

Harun-al-Raschid, why have you done this?
My own happiness is now yours!
Rome is yours! All the Empire is yours!
You say: *Abbas. He is my sign*

of love. The war with us is over.
I shall protect your Jerusalem.
Abbas stays with you, you who sent me
northern dogs more daring than lions.

ROLAND BEFORE RONCEVAUX

Ah. What a luxury to be a Moor!
I am so bored with my life as it is.
If only I could change
this daily drudgery of eight to four,
of oiling my hauberk and my sword,
of hoping for some war

to soothe this aching in my brain. Ah. War
is hard, but this is worse than any wound a Moor
can give. He's real. His sword
will glitter when it's raised. His falchion is
hand-forged by damascenes. To stand before
such a weapon can change

the blood and nerves of every Frank, can change
his fear of God to love of Holy War
and what he's striving for,
Christ Incarnate. At least the profane Moor
provides a man with certainties. As is,
my Durendal, my sword

in danger of rusting, my bloodless sword
stays taut yet brittle as those massive chains
on Uncle Charles's
suspension bridge in Mainz: I wait for war,
again to feel, again to face a fiery Moor
and split him into four.

How dull this strife. But what it must be for
Marsile and those others in his sord-
id crowd of pagan Moors

defies all imagining. What a change
their constant orgy from our steady war
on excess pleasure is!

And as for our rear guard, whose safety is
my charge, our dreary trudge north heretofore
is as noisy as a war,
but clacking hooves don't ring like clashing swords.
My back and legs are sore. I've little chance
for glory anymore.

My life is ordinary now: The more
I grease my sword, the more it feels like war,
just waiting for a change.

BEFORE THE BANQUET

where also he will find Gisela,
a tender beauty, their sister
—Theodulf of Orleans

I would skip a week of radishes
for just an evening with that young man
who stares, then laughs at me, so fondly
when the court gathers to pay homage
     and dine with Father.

You must know him, Berta — don't scold me —
you must notice his sleek, supple flanks
tighten in his bow, how turbulent
his neck muscles when he nods at me,
     his eyes that luster.

Don't summon me to a nunnery, sweet
Berta. I too much want to live,
to dress up in madras forever,
to stand very, very near to them,
     the men who flatter

so, if they're balding or odorous,
wrapping enormous hands around me.
Gascon perfumes and Father always
keep me. You won't stop me from dancing.
     I can imagine

more aging ambassadors, more hands,
more pipe and lute music, more brute dogs
crowding the Great Hall in nights to come
and I shall have it all. This, sister, is
     where I belong, but

I would sacrifice these small pleasures
one night to hear that young man whisper
"Gisela, Gisela. Will you make
love with me?" My very heart trembles.
　　There. Father's calling.

THE ORGAN IN AACHEN CATHEDRAL

*Much legend has been associated with this
instrument which was said to have had such
a soft and sweet tone that a woman died in
transports of ecstasy on hearing it.*
　　　　　　　W. L. Sumner, The Organ

Where does this music take us, Alcuin?
　　　　Backward to the Greeks
or Latins who would understand
its moan but not its melody?
　　　　Or, into the land
Saxon Widukind rules, who speaks
a tongue like ours but who can't see
　　　how different from sin

is music?　Both of us have felt our strengths
　　　　weaken, on those mute
cold nights when only fires broke
that bitter quiet where we camped.
　　　The same winds that stoke
fires the Arabians transmute
from air to bellows which are clamped
　　　to long brass pipes, whose lengths

are altered to create this roar of sound —
　　　　frightening even the Franks
who feared nothing before except
thunder rolls — with awful grace,
　　　like Ajax who stepped
to battle never giving thanks
to his gods, or like Boniface
　　　whose echoes can be found

in your own students' chanting even now.
            Alcuin, my friend
and teacher, you have shown me why
the moon changes its shape and taught
            me to multiply;
I ask you — do you apprehend
what purpose music serves for thought
        or feeling? Listen how

those booming tones reverberate below,
            clattering the walls,
till suddenly the organist
will lift his fingers, close the stops
            and clinch in a twist
the air of angels! It enthralls
this old man's heart — until it drops
        because I want to know

if it is dangerous to think about
            other worlds than ours,
when I am subject to a song,
what, if invisible these pleasures
            do move me, is wrong
with granting this machine its powers
to change my mind by aural measures
        it leaves me still in doubt.

ON THE BACK OF EINHARD'S MANUSCRIPT ON THE LIVES OF ST. PAUL AND ST. MARCELLINUS

What's the use? Do
as I may, lightning still strikes,
comets bleed across the night skies
and Louis's wars rage
and destroy the work of little men
like me, no matter what we intend
to bypass such
folly. It is wasted time I spend.

My poor heart looks to the south and flies
to some cold future
or past, but who cares?
I would cast off all that's on these pages
were I not to think, *passion,* and find
comfort there.

*

Again the hour is late.
My eyes ache from these low-burning torches.
Again Imma sleeps
restlessly. In the garden
last year's hyacinths bloom.
Soon, tomorrow night, from Seligenstadt
I will take this last work to Aachen.

What I wanted to write
is somehow still missing, but I lack
the spirit to master it. Soon
Imma will be dead. I have
given my life to a king, two saints,
and her. Summer is upon us.

OTTO III, ON ENTERING CHARLEMAGNE'S TOMB, 1000 A.D.

They buried here the age but not the man.
They draped his crown and armor with this pall
but life goes on, still doing what it can.

I've tried to emulate his stern command,
but I am born too late. After its fall
they buried here the age, and not a man

or king, Capetian, Dane or Allemand,
can resurrect the Frankish rule of Gaul.
Our lives go on; we're doing what we can.

But in this marble tomb the black-gloved hand
gripping the sceptre, the torso broad yet tall
(as though a buried angel, not a man),

the leathery body, ironclad and tanned,
the hair and nails, each grown into a ball,
the life gone on, still doing what it can,

all, all are signs that Charlemagne had planned
this silent greeting in this silent hall,
and buried here, the age is not the man
whose life goes on still doing what it can.

II

"Where were you born, cook?"

*"'Hind de hatchway, in a ferry boat, goin'
ober de Roanoke."*

*"Born in a ferry boat! That's queer, too.
But I want to know what country you were born
in, cook?"*

*"Didn't I say de Roanoke country?" he cried,
sharply.*

*"No, you didn't, cook; but I'll tell you what
I'm coming to, cook. You must go home and
be born over again; you don't know how to
cook a whale-steak yet."*

—Moby-Dick

IN NICE

When Charlemagne hit the Côte d'Azur
even the poets shuddered.
"Would he, could he touch sand?"
they asked in their rondeaus.
The Carleton clerk wrote his sister:
"Who next, the Pope?"

We rented a Fiat from Normandy
and drove without stopping.
I think the people are prettiest
not in Nice but in Cannes
where we went and wondered
is there love,

we and the poets, that is.
Again:
>Charlemagne in sandals
>under the cabaña
>twisted his mustache
>to sigh and say,
>"Ah, the British are *so* British."
>No simple Celt has feet like his.
>As a timid American
>with little humor, I
>can vouch for that,
>and if I imagine
>the hair on his chest,
>some day it may turn white.

THE FLIGHT FROM EUROPE

Another time has other lives to lead.
—*W. H. Auden*

I. Nocturne in F. Minor

Charlemagne, his ears plugged up
with Chopin, glides like a mazurka
over the white heavens spreading below.
Demigods dance on the wings in his head.
 "This is not Greek air," he jots down.
 "This is Pan American," he hears,
 "This is your pilot speaking,
 that on your lap is *quiche lorraine,*
 that on your left is northern Spain,
 if you must know the stewardess' name,
 you must disturb her — just buzz her.
 Have a pleasant flight."

Charlemagne is out of his armor
in a minute,
 he refuses the news-
papers, like any good tease,
he strips her instead, eyes
rise like the comets darting
across Miss Susan's pinned lapel.
Miss Susan dreams of the stars
kissing in the in-flight movie.
The white heavens spread

suddenly open:
 "To plunge into an ocean," (crescendo)
 "Eternal ocean and we in a lead box."

I order a second vodka tonic
to wag it over Chopin.
 "Helen, let me blot thy thighs! O."

The ink runs on his notebook, Miss
Susan smiles, not politely, Miss
Susan brings him his red wine
with another vodka tonic coming.

II. Crossing the Bar

"We are all in this together,"
someone whispers, it is
Socrates upstairs
in seven four seven flight
two two two.
Parmenides on the white piano
tickles the ivories for Edith Piaf.
Thales drinks whiskey like it's
water:
        "You should see old Anaximenes gasp
        when they flash the no smoking,"
he laughs and shifts his fat.
Empedocles coughs, the air-
conditioning
conditioning
                while Charlemagne
a man always in his element
orders a blanket and more wine.

III. By the Dawn's Early Light

Charlemagne has taken the plunge.
Miss Susan tucks him in and runs
a polished finger over his lips.
I prepare for a lunar eclipse.
The Nocturne in F Minor ends:

As I write this
I am leaving the continent.
I am tired of it anyway.
It's very late, though soon
it may be early, or, as
Eliot says:
          If all time is eternally present,
          All time is unredeemable.
All time is unredeemable.
We are up in the air
at the still turning point
of the world of the world.
Somehow Heraclitus,
stout Heraclitus,
found heaven down there
                        in a river.

IV. Vaguely Realizing Westward

We put away our notebooks
pending our arrival. Miss
Susan assures us:
     "The United States has
     a beauty all its own."
I love you
          says Charlemagne
as he finishes his breakfast.

V. A Song of Gesture

Bearded, dog-tired Charlemagne
burns his tongue on Miss Susan's
coffee

as we descend, fall
flat, the runway approaches,
rises like some prophet's message:
        "Refresh me! Fetch me!
        Keep encouraged, I am waiting!"
Our bird grabs with its tires
the white lines between the red
flagged ramparts, trees and bushes
writhe — we are a European hurricane
arriving:
        "I rose obsolete,
        figured in majolica,
        penetrated space, but eggs
        for breakfast and I am
        waiting fired up."

Unfasten your belts, folks! We've landed!

A sandy Hollywood pioneer, bearded
Charlemagne squints at the sun.
Our Greek friends are off to find
their baggage:
        "Where's the men's room and a shave?"
It's near morning in New York,
music water piped into the air-
port and people kissing hello.
        "You have twenty-nine years
        with a passport, thank you."

One step past customs,

                        Charlemagne,
what a magnificent beast, at home,
how do you do
how do you do
                welcome.

CHARLEMAGNE AT MACY'S

My darlings,
I simply haven't the time
to write this one. Besides,
the only peculiar part
shows Charlemagne on the sidewalk
staring down that blind accordion player.

I remember. It might have been
yesterday:
> Staring down that blind accordion
> player, staring at his whiskers,
> his red eyes, the strand of hair
> cross the forehead, wool cap, etc.,
> Charlemagne marveled, "Our beards,
> our jawbones!" He brought his hand
> to his chin, he rarely does that:
> "Remarkably similar! Remarkable!"
> But we just hurried past and. . .

MARTIAL ARTS

When the massive, xylographic door of the Philadelphia
            Museum of Art blew shut it was up to me to
            pry it open again but I was in a deep rut
            floundering in underground acrylics.
"Shove it!" Charlemagne echoed across the gallery's centuries
            of cracked oils and dried-up aquarelles.
I tried, planned an attack, asked a sentry Rembrandt had
            propositioned once to guide me through that
            wartorn beaux arts territory but the silly rigid
            soldier wouldn't take the charge and stood
brave but listlessly defeated.

I retreated to tell my pathetic story to the king, imbibing,
            muscles flexed, Dürer's woodcuts of the saints.
He was lying on the floor but he rises whenever he speaks:
            "You say your task is destructive that it breaks
            who knows how many hundreds of years how
            many hundreds of hard-working hearts that you
            are ashamed that within you there lurks despite
            what you know to be good in the arts a nausea,
            and all because it's stuffy in here and you want
            to let in fresh air."
Charlemagne loosened his bolo tie and the sweat on his neck
            beaded around his collar leaving a smear.
With our hat-check ticket to the check-out he rushed me but
            before we could pay a single dollar I stumbled
            over a live electric wire by the cuff of my shaggy
            pants which greatly embarrassed the feline
            Egyptian statues standing preciously near.

This meant war. (I embraced the counter girl.)

Security guards descended in small swarms ringing alarms and
        bringing a crowd and a curator into the middle
        of harm's way while old King Carlon fought
        them off like a dog with an armory of paper
        clips and I protected our rear with our raingear,
        aegis umbrella, New England lobsterman's
        broadbrimmed Northeasterner's cap.
The bold but dull American arts of the nineteenth century
        suddenly blew up in a chaotic swirl a few
        Napoleons flew out into corners Braques fell
        from its meathook Albers suffered an indenta-
        tion and the curator lost his brandy his book
        his nap and the *New York Times'* prized
        commendation.
Outnumbered by seven of them to a man we grabbed our
        galoshes and ran off.

BREAKFAST: OFF THE SUNNYSIDE EXIT

"I could eat a horse," he said then turned
the headlights down. One of those back road nooks
where coffee drips with cigarettes, where vans
and tractor trailers block the parking lot.
A view? "If Henry Ford were driving by,
we wouldn't even see him," Charlemagne
acknowledged. I industriously referred
him to the bill of fare, excused myself.
(The trip to dawn was endless.) "Hotcakes, eggs,
and ham, not boiled, please," requested Chaz,
"and for my friend, the Pennsylvania Blue
Plate Special, dish of extra toast, not burned,
and make that juice tomato."
                              Off the books,
I don't like other people making plans
for me when I am in the toilet. Not
that he was lacking grace, but how you fry
an egg is crucial to Americans.
Imagine my despair when I incurred
my *chota hazri* "over easy."
                              Self-
possessed, I bit down hard on the coffee dregs.
"The Rambler's not much faster than an ass,"
I said, "but one can't eat it." And he: "That's true."

EDIFICE REX

your first cry at the prairie's door
— Hart Crane

I. Wheeling, Crestline, Gary

I speak as one who lives here. Charlemagne,
a tourist incognito, has applied
for socio-cultural asylum. Jane,
the one in glasses, put affairs aside

to travel with us, cross the countyline:
a new *ménage à trois.* The nights are best;
when Charlemagne is driving, Jane goes blind,
and I down the dim turnpike (as you guessed)

to look for what I haven't found in years,
for Joe Dimaggio, for Moby-Dick,
for El Dorado Ranch, and now, for Sears
and Roebuck's catalogue, turning this trick:

The magic in this nation comes in parts
to be assembled piece by piece at home
with glue, with nails, with teeth, with Jane, with arts
precisely detailed. Where? Inside the tome

they call *Directions for Assembly.* O,
I need new directions for this assembly.
It's five A.M., King Chaz still on the go,
his long hair flowing, buckles on his knee;

Jane looks to me for vision, fast asleep;
I still can't put it all together, yet
riding, gliding, Charlemagne might leap
or scale this mystery I call a threat.

30

II. The Sears Tower

Skidmore, Owings, Merrill,
Lynch, Pierce, Fenner, Smith
chime in all men's choirs.
Cubed within these walls with
ears that pop, stop, open,
the three of us are rising
one hundred seven stories
while penned in I am sizing
up the situation,
                    but Charlemagne,
keen as any high-toned dog, grabs Jane
to say he can't believe his eyes. I know
what's next by instinct: these new buildings grow
bigger babies in the bank. But we arrive
on top. (What do I write? Spirits revive
at one thousand three hundred fifty-three feet?
Salvation here?) "Can't you be more discreet?"
Chaz blurts; a midwesterner steps on his toe:
"Thank you for not smoking." So I go
into the gift shop. (What to buy for friends
downtown? What will be saved when this trip ends?)

People say, "Look at that view!" We look at that view,
obedient and gray. (I put my thumb on you,
railroads and freeways.) "Then you miss the point," Charles
chants under his breath. His eyes gape at the laurels
and the lake's full-bodied blue. Chicago haunts us:
Hancock, holding its own, insures, the Standard trusts
that, brute force though he may be, Charlemagne shaking it
can't knock this joss house down on citizens making it.

III. The Tribune Tower

Inch by inch up this splendid tower
an avataric man lifts his body, hour
by hour, limb over limb, glows white
in snow, haloed by morning sunlight.
His bold flanks uncovered, Charlemagne
plants rosy fingers in stone; the chain
taut around his waist clings to the post
astride the catwalk, while down the coast

by Lake Michigan, hands in pockets,
I amble, wool cap drawn down to my eye sockets,
anticipating; my change jingles.
From his flexed advantage Chaz singles
me out from commuters who bristle
and hustle to work. At his whistle
I whirl and spot and snap a photo
of impeccable Quasimodo,

alias Charles the acrobat
on a minute scale (slightly hunched forward, no hat,
tailcoat fluttering rapidly) of
the neo-Gothic: Here is the love
of nature Ralph Emerson recounts
so fondly in his tropes, which amounts
to a series of leaps to heaven.
But Charlemagne impedes the reverend

by his own pedagogical clime,
his sheer determination and his bent in time.
Up with the sun, unheralded, warmed
by blood rising from his hips, he's stormed
this city without making headlines
or pouring oil on those below. "Good designs,"
he says, shaking the snow from his eyes,
"help us better attend to the skies."

EXPIRATION

With the moon in second quarter and the stars
reposing the Oak Park suburban sky
I take a back seat while Charlemagne eases
his hoarfrost and richly bearded body
atop the Rambler. Thick Frank Lloyd Wright bricks
hunch in little walls whose holly ivy
wreathes the sidewalk by the quiet car.
Charles shows a liking for this place:

He jockeys for position, locks his hands
behind his head, and leaning back, his knees
lifted, "Has it come to this?" he asks me.
I tactfully don't answer. Poplar trees
bow in a wishful silence the south winds
usher in, and the traffic desists
with deference. I nod for Jane to see.
He clears his throat: "Hmp-hm, it's come to this

moment of time, the world I knew before.
Even after Rome I never felt
such peace or satisfaction; never more
is one alive than when embracing death.
This evening is today's palladium,
or elephant, or mare, or loyal Celt —
a rare treasure. What would this life become
never were a man to lose his breath?"

MILWAUKEE'S CLEAN

Jane and I
burned ourselves
out buying
groceries

(O to fondle your thighs
over frozen french fries),

gallons of
gas and the
six-pack of
postcards.

Dear Byron (he writes)
Milwaukee's a clean place
with postcards to show you
how big it is —
how big Allegra must be! —
and Greek wars you can imagine
have touched us here:
delicatessens close,
dogs (bless their hearts) bark less.
We stay behind you, dear
friend, but forgive us;
we are not Europe anymore.

I went to the racetrack.
Horses here all run
in the same direction, daily
double: A wrinkled woman
in a green kerchief came to me,
her face bleeding,

knuckles chewed to the bone,
to ask me for a dime:
"I don't beg, fella, I work.
I was winning but forgot
I was hungry."
Hungry, I thought,
and this is Milwaukee,
town of towns, unreal
sanitary city, Byron,
O I must miss you
or I wouldn't wish for you
as I do so often.
            Salud to Athens!

On the way to Wauwatosa,
I asked him about it:
        "If you can, John,
        don't run away from yourself,
                    or from history,
                    or from old movies."

THE MACULA

I caught Jane kissing
Charlemagne underneath
the mistletoe that night.

I was drunk and dancing
an old soft-shoe medley
while visions of sugarplums

crowded the smoke-filled
studio efficiency,
spinning like a discus;

a nausea leapt up like gas
in my throat, stale wine
in my nose and out

through the decked halls,
up on the rooftop, heaven
sighed in the silence

among the bus fumes.
I coughed at the penthouses
and my huffy cheeks blew out

like slit tires, ears split
like hubcaps, lips bitter
with the rubber taste of the city.

The night before Christmas
wind restoring my head
to its shoulders, I thought

about apartment life.
But she had kissed him
and I had seen it, all

in all, for the love
of truth, had stared at them
as at a car accident, or

at Michelangelo's Adam's
finger, or at the star of David,
and the centuries became

suddenly real,
or, at least, more common
than the smell of my own body.

CHARLES ON THE TICKET

I love to be in America.
— *Stephen Sondheim*

After forty-eight hours in Omaha
we began to smell
the beef of the northern Platte.

So long, so long
the Rambler was parked
near a pretty little pink
Chevrolet, that grillwork grinning
it violated meter
and lured the local police.

Jane put her head on my chest
to console. (An "O" for the odor
of woman and woes.) Yet
I'm still not one with complaint
or appeal, you won't find much meat
on these bones. I am a mere
mental diversion in an otherwise
hunky America.

So Charles sank his teeth
into this, like every,
human situation,
                    and soon
out of court, out of town,
out of mind, he had paid our debt
to society.

PRECIPICE PIECE

Mid-March a faulty alternator broke
us down outside a small Wyoming town
near Devil's Tower, but I was not about
to scrap the Rambler here, so though the ground
was ice, I crawled under the hood to think,
while Jane wrote notes on magazine covers
to friends in Crestline, and Charles over maps
pored, his eyes looking for a route, and spoke:
"Cheer up, Saxon. You'll get to know the ropes."
I rubbed my pants with axle grease. Chaz winked
at Jane, pretending not to notice my
grimace; a nut and bolt let out a SLAM
and tumbled to the road. "We'll have it towed,"
the king suggested. Colder than a clam
I left for help but heard the Rockies singing:

THE SONG OF THE AMERICAN AUTOMOBILE ASSOCIATION

Well a man named Jo from Buffalo
drove a two-ton pick-up truck.
When he reached Elk Pass, plumb out of gas
he was and plumb out of luck.

Well he cursed this fact and he spat tobac-
co from his fat cheek so to say,
"What a goddam fix! Here in the sticks
I am and where's Triple A?"

> *Well it's A. A. A.,*
> *that regiment of rotomotion,*
> *on heel, o'er dale, or by the ocean,*
> *friend to men where least predicted,*
> *saviour of the sore afflicted*
> *car: go, go, Triple A.*

Well this Jo our man he had a plan
so he stuck out his thumb and groaned
till an Oldsmobile stopped short on that heel
and said, "Right thar blows a phone."

Well he dropped a dime and he heard it chime
"Hello! Can we help today?"
"Well my truck broke down," said Jo with a frown.
"Don't fret, son. We're Triple A."

> *Refrain*

Well our good ol' boy he glowed with joy
when that red tow truck appeared.
As they pumped the gas, the elk on Elk Pass
applauded and so did the deer.

Well old Jo was pleased to see the ease
with which he would reach L.A.,
and the whole trip long one helluva a song
he sang for the Triple A.

> *Refrain*

APPROACHING CARIBOU

And hence we three henchmen walked forth
awhile, our ears made sensitive
by a cold but open reception
    in the wind.

And in the far, sleeping valleys sheep
ignored the sheepskin wrapped around me
stumbling to Mammoth Springs, Charlemagne
    in the lead.

And swifter than Halley's Comet, he
bit through to that northern aurora,
two days and without a bunion, stalked
    in the hills,

and he took to that trail like an ox,
and he whistled in French at the blue
wide sky, turned up pages of my Pound
    in the night,

and comforted Jane there, saying "Babe,"
buckling the collar of her parka,
"when I think of silent caribou
    in the north

and of my late, ancient companions,
you will be among them."
Since I overheard this, I wrote it
    in the book

and without the canny king's consent
my own thoughts strayed to the caribou
valiant, keeping their stride majestic
    but distant.

DOWN THE SNAKE RIVER

Down Henry's Fork where the river spray's jet white
waters chopping icy tears on my blue wrists
slick back my hairs, colder in this air of foam
than under the hard wake left by my yellow
innertube, I through my orange life jacket
clutch at my ragged intestines and lie flat
like a thwart, scull caught under my chin, the jerk
of the rapid current underneath slapping,
thwacking the wood against my cheek, and the sky —
emptied by the winds that carry it — the sky
an azure gloom.
                    I think of my childhood
but scarcely, as here I lie, American
Falls to our south, rapidly approaching us,
as geniculated rocks buffet the arch
in my back, as the spit gurgling in my throat
splits my concentration on the loping sky,
as I like a gosling careen from my boat
and fly where the osprey off the banks scatter
far into the patched face that is the forest
and release a long, round, desperate, and dry
moan.
           I am alone and I'm dreaming of sex,
yet next to me away they float from these lines
into the violence of a spasmodic day.
I know like the chamois mindlessly
staring out from behind the trees what I see
but don't know how to say it:

                    Jane's leg dangles
from the side of their bark canoe, her bared thighs
snow white, her knees raised like miniature mountains,
as Charlemagne guides them through this writhing stream.
I press my preserver closer to my chest,
my body skids faster than the blood in my head,
rushing down the line, rushing into the Snake,
my eyes go blank. I am a wreck, utterly.

REGARDS

She is no Calamity Jane,
this gangbuster writing
on complimentary stationary
in Pocatello, Idaho, later.

She remembers the young doctor
in Crestline, her first night
after making love on the edge
of the Sandusky River:

"I rolled on the forest floor
like a black-and-white kitten
in yarn, to keep myself warm
when the bloodlines were low,"

Or, "I knit my own kneesocks now."
Propped up in a hardwood bed,
to the doctor she sends
her blessings, to a poet

who brought her roses once
she sends her blessings,
to the women, men, and children
who live within their means

she sends her compliments
gushing, inspired, promising
like hot water geysers, but
as she stumbles to the bathroom,

she meets herself in the mirror
and contorts her perfervid

but fine facial lines, saying,
"You are no calamity, Jane,

but rather an old faithful now."
"If it takes my life," she adds,
"if it takes my life some day,
I'll write a song to the old man."

STOPPING BY WELLS, NEVADA

There's nothing unexpected here, but me:
the red hills swell, the desert cracks in veins
the blood bursts in my pumping blistered temples

the sun singes my hair to scalded sagebrush
flattened by the rattlesnakes, without
an end, the road winding around the hills

the hills winding across the orange plain
where there is no water but only rock
where hearts are burned, where souls and bones are heaped

where spirits come to cavemouths into hell
where thirst, starvation, heat and we go on
where Charlemagne yawns, Jane draws trees, and I:

I'd rather stop awhile, I'd rather sleep.

IN THE MISSION AND PRODUCE DISTRICT,
SAN FRANCISCO

I must not be the genius
Charlemagne thought I was buying me
out in the streets among cantelope crates
and tomato warehouses to write.
I was thinking of changing my sex
or my species from Homo sapiens
to a purely canine variety
or to that breed of messenger pigeon
who pecks about snatching for scraps here
from the heads of the non-union lettuce.

"You shall not go hungry, man," he said,
digging with his aureate hands for change.
"I want to be your divan poet;
I am the profit in your pocket," I said,
but I hadn't a penny to spare. There
like lira in black Turkish markets
I turned dusky and faded as Pandarus,
lecher, sapper of animal juices,
a mammary man with sagging breasts,
who gathers catalogues, junk mail, rare coins,

but "You're not yet twenty-nine" I was told
by a man who was king at thirty,
who never heard of the word *Europe,*
ignored signals of his own death,
drank only in moderation, a man
in league with the heart, and in front of it
his face on a thousand medallions.
What a future he stocked up for me,
a ghost writer with a bone to chew.
One day they'll make me a postage stamp.

VARIOUS SACRIFICES

Toes and elbows at cross purposes
Chaplin Charlie hangs
                    silently
from the wall of this west coast snackette
as bucko Charlemagne tosses
his familiar glance at the postboard.

Two are at odds: Jane
wants to drive to the cinema but
      "I haven't had my snack yet,"
(I've fasted since we left Big Sur)
      "and I'm not about to give it up
      here in buena Ventura" and rush to
and gush in my lemonade,
as though it were liquid gold and I
a prospector, dry without hope.

      "Forgive me, sir," begs Charlemagne
of Pablo Francisco, the soda clerk,
      "but who is that man on the wall?"
      "A very funny man, señor" is all.

      "Let's go to the movies!"
chirps irritant Jane, scraping
Pacific sand from her knees.
I throw her the crust from my sour dough
saying,
      "Take. Eat."
She refuses, like any good tease, hands
coupled behind her back, and wanders
mildly up to the wall, to sigh and say,

"Chaplin was a victim of the talkies."

She looks to his softening eyes
cast in the black-and-white placard,
and even-minded Charlemagne
offering his bowl of alphabet soup
    says
        nothing.

THREE HOURS IN LOS ANGELES

1

After waiting in a line
for the sun to go down
we enter like the stars
enter the Universe.
Red flashlight in hand
Charon tears our tickets
to usher us cross the plush
burgundy carpet to our box
where we watch a world premiere.

"Americans fear their own
sensuality," I whisper as a hush
succumbs the crowd; we clap;
the eyes do not breathe but
are quiet, without fanfare,
crying, *feel for me, feel for me.*
Jane drops her hand in Charles's lap.
The curtain rises on a take
of the twentieth century fox:

His elegant paw he places
inside her butter-blonde thigh
and I in wonder look on them,
her scarlet cheeks, blue eyes,
turbulent lips, hand caressing
his forehead. How I ache
for them to kiss. His voice
and her smile are stunning,
their veil of desire, sacred.

My misery is the misery
of angels, of bringing hell up
in the first place, of lacking
the will to act, and of singing:
Marilyn! Gable! I sigh,
where does my flesh belong?
He longs, she longs, and I,
longing for both, know only
I wish I could die.

2

Having left the theater by myself
I start my cunning car and drive this fable
south on one-o-one. This decadence
will seize our day, I think, unless we're able
to leave it behind, not to look back,
to say we're either older or we're not,
short on the old comforts.
I didn't want to tangle in this knot
of infidelity, but here I am —
no lion's courage in my lion's heart.
When I appeal to Pluto, I'll be damned
if I must throw away my human part.
No one tells a poet how to live,
least of all, his demon. I'm amative
by nature, one who gets around, not good
yet friend to beasts. We all struggle to keep
above ground, but desire cries give me food.
As I exit from the freeway, I go deep.

3 At Pershing Square

I re-enter this netherworld alone
and loiter at the Olive Ave. bus stop
outside the Pacific Mutual Life & Savings
in which the rich men simmer.
I watch the homosexuals in the park.
The Philharmonic Hall has undergone
repairs, so Adventists can praise the dead.

A chic Chicano passes me a buck.
He wants to share a coffee, have me, black.
"Bug out," I want to say, but I'm alone
and can't shape the words.
A dense smog lowers as I cross the dark
and halfway up the sidewalk halt, my head

pounding with artillery fire, flak
exploding in my brain. The petty cash
I'm clutching in my pocket with my life
slowly turns my palm green.
But by the statue, in a noxious dream
I holler flatly, "Lafayette, I'm here."
"All wars are boyish," Herman Melville said.

ROUND ABOUT MIDNIGHT

"Inside," says Charlemagne
as he dons his own black shades
to lead us into the devil's lair
of Miles Davis, John Coltrane
and all that jazz: Parmenides
picks out a breezy tune on his white
piano, while Miles lax
as a satin doll, eyes green,
with red hot lips, fades

in favor of Coltrane's sax
blending his tenor with ease.
Trane suffers the blues tonight
yet I, though timid, am not remiss
of the eloquence of air,
so flushed with a love supreme
I offer Jane a kiss.

ARIZONA AUBADE

I am larger than I thought.
—Walt Whitman

We're a hell of a long way from Phoenix.
We must burn those miles, beat the track to
Santa Fe. The manifest has seen its
better days, Walt Whitman. Step down back to

old Los Alamos, years ago when
buffalo and bandelier were wild.
(Albuquerque ruled real Indians then.)
Listen: Drop your ocean dream awhile.

East, young man, go east. Forget the sunsets
and their uttered darkness. No emotions
prattle like the yearnings in our own hearts
rusting out from overuse; no potions

magically revive us. It's a long way,
bomb or no bomb, open roads be blasted,
going straight to go in circles, to say
here America rose while it lasted.

JANE TAKES A VACATION

The truth is plain
            and the concrete
laid across the state road
                        is the same
which is why grown men build highways
where there's no one
            save a few golddiggers
            scorpions or snakes.
People like to think
                        they know
                        what they're doing.
That's the whole of it, plain, flat,
hard as a rock because it's just that,
                        a rock
overrun by occasional rabbits
or westcoast bound rusted autos
                        racing into the sky,
                        clear, round, blue, fat
against the rock

            as our veins are
            before they burst
                        from our hearts.

Jane, for one, knew this
            and for that
she turned her eyes still further south
                        below Truth
or Consequences. Away from me, away from Chuck.
She rolled up her pack, licked her lips
                        which were chapped
                        from the taste of adventure,
                                    and with that

she stuck out her thumb;
                    the immediate landscape
          reacted.
Charlemagne spat (on the side of the road)
and a truck interrupted its run
                    to give her a ride
                    on its back.
Jane made some time in Las Cruces but said,
          "Meet me in El Paso, Jack"
which I did.

THE DEAD DUDE

1

I buckled my greenjeans and spurs
and pulled back the curtains. The curs
(no deer, no antelope) lopped
in the dust and growled, so I cropped
    my hair with my hand

and felt for my gun. It was gone.
The sun through the window at dawn
from Charley, asleep but intact,
drew blood to his cheeks. I lacked
    a hat with a band,

a suitable holster, and the words
to start off this day, and the herds
of longhorns relaxing had wrought
discouragement here where I'd sought
    a home on the range.

"How strange," I thought, "this Rome is,
where cowboys do nothing but comb
their oil slick locks. Where there's smoke
there are cigarettes, sausage, and folk
    enough, but how strange

that I haven't met with the breed
who rifle or murder. Indeed,"
I sighed as I curried my vest,
"how awkward I am in the West
    with only a pen."

As if there were whiskey on his breath,

the red-bearded Charlemagne stretched,
his jawbone unraveling: "John,"
he said, as he strapped on his gun,
    "You're at it again."

He led me downstairs to the street
where, counting to ten in the heat,
he said, "You have everything, yet
you always want more than you get."
    I started to sweat.

        2

So I looked him straight
in his lunate eye, saying,
"You can say that again,"

but in my position, flat
on my back, it did not
bear repeating, he thought.

So Charley blew blue smoke
from the tip of his silver gun
and moseyed out of town.

By sunset Jane came and broke
into tears, saying,
"You are such a clown,

always on the run,
never slowing down, then
thinking it your fate

as a poet diplomat
or Sunday redeemer to put
in your mouth your foot."

3

I am turning my back
and I am turning back

but I can see myself
now, pacific mirror,

for the coward I was
when that rude gun approached

that quiet mesquite plain
near El Paso, friendly.

I was lost, coming to,
after our flight, the Rio Grande

yet say: Here, Jane, we are
what we are when we are

no longer. I am learning
now as the Hopi did

so I am turning back
to see another side

of the moon. I am turning
back on myself, on what I said

before, when the soil was fertile
for me, not for others.

I am turning back to a space
where time is not an essence

somewhere ahead of us
where the elements govern.

4

Like a dog I dug my bones from underground
and up I picked my body, selfishly
insisting by my silence I was sound
and fit to go on living, not to be
the tumbleweed or villain of this peace,
or gray-faced mutt who's undefined, defying
the human frontier laws: I faced the east
and saw there one I knew, and stopped him, crying,

"Stetson!" (But here's a change.) He tipped his hat,
"good morning" said, according to his rule,
and flexed his holstered hips to shift his fat,
laughing: "You are a reasonable fool
assembled on these plains, but to endure,
my roving frère, your gestures must be pure."

FOOTLIGHTS

Of the wide screen and of the epic:

Charlemagne, his name secondary here,
fades into the llaño,
all salt flats and sagebrush,
on the back of a castrated horse.
Is he limping, or
is it the camera?

If I say my mind is chaos,
do you see stars sprouting
from my eyes and ears?
Or do you see tears?

Charles, bastard,
I've lost you:
    you come straight through my legs
    until I need to swallow
    or to vomit
my saliva,
and you — what you've left me,
and Jane — her hair grown yellow,
and me,
and my health.

Your old horse must die now.
You must limp yourself, the
lecher you want to be —
I will sleep on you then,
    like any good wife,
all salts, flats, and sagebrush.
I will cry into your boy's tit.
I will cry.

CONFEDERATES' PARK

Squatting on the steps in her blue shorts Jane
at the Memphis Public Library is
skimming a book by Martin Buber, *Ich
und Du.* A brilliant sun is up on this day,
throwing power out like yellow fever.

We are not a theater for the absurd
nor is the prairie schooner any more
a valid means of transport than the mule
with forty acres of private dust
Jane might've known a hundred years ago

is: We for a time have sacked the Rambler
to bask in this sun, but, as usual,
I am worried over Reconstruction,
more liable to preen the museums
with artifacts than to bother to see

what to Charlemagne is a civil war:
As Buber addresses her memory
burned Jane, absorbed, scratches her inner thigh,
while the king, my friend, lies down in the grass
trimmed like his summer beard but still deep green.

"You are in another world," she tells him,
with which with human dexterity he
putting his lips on her inner thigh cools
what the sun has made of her there.
I wonder how we'll ever settle down.

THROUGH ASHEVILLE SLOWLY

Through Asheville slowly, till well after three,
King Charles, in smoking jacket, walked with me.
All night the steamy, sodden streets before us
unrolled like long, wet tongues, from which a chorus
of church chimes echoed at the quarter hours.

I raged and rattled on about the powers
of words. The air grew warmer. Then I wept
as griffins, basilisks and demons leapt
from every alley.
                Charles took my arm,
then reassured me they would do no harm.
I said, "I don't know what I'm doing here."
"There's nothing, then," he said, "nothing to fear."

AT LAST CHANCE MOTEL

Her green eyes whistled and my eyes came
unglued, as she (Jane) lightly dipped
from the chlorine water her knees
to which her chin was allocated
        deftly by the pool.

I sensed our aging Charlemagne, mellow
in our bathing presence, stroke
his marvelous chin, a grin only
his silence breaking. I spoke and nodded,
        nodded and spoke

of her skin, her sauterne hair, our future
bliss and my obvious hope:
my wish for a house with a child
or a job in Virginia. After a sip
        on her wet gin and tonic

Jane resumed hugging her browning calves,
clinging like halves of a whole
body, with the intimate touch of a *pas
de deux,* her toes arched at the blue
        below. "To Roanoke," I said,

"To Roanoke we must go. . ." and from there
in my upper left neck a muscle
where the king asleep on his red faldstool
could not fathom its bloody depths
        cringed, with my soul.

THE END OF THE LINE

The old man was dreaming about lions.
— *Ernest Hemingway*

Not far from North Carolina
just south of the Chesapeake Bay
aboard a continental yacht
seventeen days from our last stop
a hop, skip, and jump from Kitty Hawk
in the three-thirty weltered sun
after a late lunch of oysters,
omelettes, and sherry, in red trunks
drawn to his waist by elastic,
shirtless, with a monogrammed cross
hanging from his neck, white lotion
smudging the thick hair on his chest,
his beard grown gray at the temples,
just before snoozing, the sherry
weighing heavy in the nostrils,
body leaning back, spreadeagled
on the turquoise canvas deck chair
between consciousness and a long yawn,
brawny, sunburned, sunglassed Charlemagne

felt a slight tug on his trawler.
(I paused from salting a blue-point.)

Whatever it was disappeared.
The white-caps resurged knowingly.
Maybe it will return again
flounder, tuna, marlin, shark, whale,
    but Jane, removing her sandals,
    and I, ending what I'd begun,
    by our presence witnessed a change
    in this history: Charlemagne

reeled in, baited his hook once more,
cast, smiled, lifted his glasses,
slapped his knee, winked at us, and said,
"Of the styles of catching fish,
the big one always gets away."

EVENSONG

After turning it over once or twice
I put a finished product on your plate.
In our back yard, surrounded by good friends,
forsythias, occasional flies, and food,
we sit with plastic knives and forks to eat
in silence. Thomas sips a Napa wine,
Virginia brushes butter on her corn,
you slice the bread you baked this morning, I
adjust the dial on the radio
so we can listen to the World Series,
and dusk again transforms our little town
from concrete blocks, compounded in the dust,
to fields of household light that rise to heaven.
But suddenly, static, and a voice:

"We interrupt the struggle in your life
to share an oddly special bulletin
from the far side of the moon. Charlemagne,
the first lieutenant monarch cast in space,
en route to Jupiter, has spotted some
thing — rising cross the asteroids. He thinks
it's a comet with a message, or
perhaps, a Danish king who's gone berserk;
he can't detail precisely its design
but promises to keep his eye on it;
his voice was fading, but we heard him say,
God keep me from completing anything.
When further words were garbled, just a song
came through. Now back to local programming."

A gap.
        The charcoal smell pervades the air.
The family dog draws closer for his bone.
"Immortality belongs to others,"
I grin aloud, but no one seems to hear
me or the radio. A whack. A cheer.
I turn the volume up. Another cheer.
(Charlemagne, if he were here, would know
exactly what's important in this game —
the pitcher's earned run average or the strength
of this hitter.) A long fly. It's a homer.

I ask you, finally, "Is the steak too rare?"
Munching, you take my hand.
                  Our human breed
wants constantly but consciously to thrive
so to each other we must mutually pledge
our lives, our fortunes, and our sacred honor.
We're young, dear Jane. Let's plant a mutant seed.

Available from Plumbers Ink Books

Arreola, Allysia J., *Elephant Eater* (chapbook) $2.00
ISBN: 0-935684-00-X

Gery, John, *Charlemagne: A Song of Gestures* $5.95
ISBN: 0-935684-06-9

Gomes, Teresa M., *Friendly Correspondence* (chapbook) $2.00
ISBN: 0-935684-01-8

Kamei, Marlene, *Stone Lantern Essays* $4.95
ISBN: 0-935684-02-6

Kempher, Ruth Moon, *Three Ring Circus* $4.95
ISBN: 0-935684-04-2

McCallum, Tracy, *Fast Associations* $4.95
ISBN: 0-935684-03-4

When ordering, add 50¢ to help defray mailing costs.
30% discount available on orders of ten or more books.

Plumbers Ink Books
P. O. Box 233
Cerrillos, New Mexico 87010